Malak, a reader, a writer, a student, a teacher, a human, debuts *All the Colors of the Sky*—an expression of her personality, bright-colored field of vision and lyrical heart. A newborn author, with much to say and more she wonders about, shares her thoughts on this, indeed, very magical life, love, the beauty of hearts broken, the spoken and the inexplicable and all the subjects that transpire in our lives.

A collection on the mixtape of love & life

All the Colors of the Sky

Malak

Austin Macauley Publishers
LONDON · CAMBRIDGE · NEW YORK · SHARJAH

Copyright © Malak 2024

The right of **Malak** to be identified as author of this work has been asserted by the author in accordance with Federal Law No. (7) of UAE, Year 2002, Concerning Copyrights and Neighboring Rights.

All rights reserved. No part of this publication may be reproduced, stored in a retrieval system, or transmitted in any form or by any means, electronic, mechanical, photocopying, recording, or otherwise, without the prior permission of the publishers.

Any person who commits any unauthorized act in relation to this publication may be liable to legal prosecution and civil claims for damages.

The age group that matches the content of the books has been classified according to the age classification system issued by the Ministry of Culture and Youth.

ISBN – 9789948790594 – (Paperback)
ISBN – 9789948790587 – (E-Book)

Application Number: MC-10-01-2656172
Age Classification: E

Printer Name: iPrint Global Ltd
Printer Address: Witchford, England

First Published 2024
AUSTIN MACAULEY PUBLISHERS FZE
Sharjah Publishing City
P.O. Box [519201]
Sharjah, UAE
www.austinmacauley.ae
+971 655 95 202

To my family

This one's by you,
This one's for you,
As I am, all, always to you

All my love;

The Meaning of Color

All the Colors of the Sky is a collection of ten parts that holds together as one whole story of *Love and Life.*

A poetry repertoire enjoying a medley of emotions, a spectrum of tales that glitters in different light, a variety of aching thoughts and gay ones.

It is the compassionate storytelling of mankind, and the inevitability of falling in love with us.

Each Part of *All the Colors of the Sky* presents a unique shade that paints a picture of its character and tenor, a snapshot of the poetry inside.

This collection is a mixtape of *Love and Life* within ourselves and between everly skies,

A fantasy of everything beyond what meets the eyes.

All the Colors of the Sky

Where there is fantasy, there is life

Part I: I write this for you

Part II: The Time Is Love

Part III: Somethings are life

Part IV: Tales of Tongues Tied

Part V: To love—is to and fro

Part VI: All Colors of the rainbow

Part VII: The light in my eyes, The stars in the skies, The sunset and sunrise

Part VIII: Vent & Verse

Part IX: I love you, I love you, I love you ...

Part X: Forevermore;

Dear reader,

No poem would ever sound so music without an audience so musical.
Thank you for choosing to be here and being so delightful.

Welcome to
All the Colors of the Sky,

Malak.

Lavender

The color of devotion,
Unconditional love.

I write this for you

I vow to have eyes so honest in chanting Adore,
Amour

When my speaking
Is too wee and shy
When the seas finish
And shrink to the sky
When everything
And everywhere fail and lie
To give you
So freely
So eloquently
So alive

What I own of love
To the sweet of your eye,
That you are mine
Today and *to die.*

Ode One;
(16)

Two souls
two lives,
one home
different hearts.
Akin faces
kindred traces
of unlike graces,
each the lead of their races.
Afar minds
both one of a kind
in oneness intertwined,

and all that is beauty is in me with you, found.

Two souls
(17)

*W*hen brought to daylight the same hour me and you
who knew that despite our color
your pain would be mine too.

I held you tighter than the breath wavers within you
every time eyes, *blue,* accused—
how prettier I am than you.

I captured every silent tear
you hid, behind a smiling face
together all our years.

The world and its men set you and I foe
fistfight the fire I would rather undergo
than the once, *my love,* to stand rival you.

But O' that every time you win over me
in contest you and I foist enemy
all my agony, all my fear turns to glee.

Win, win, my dear, over me
love you the more *you love me,*
pay for the moment, *with my life,* I loved you less than be.

~

I unsee words
in a world seas of words
I see how you complete me.

I see the beauty
you never look to see,
I am yours and you are to me.

I know that your color makes you—*you*
and mine distinguishes me from you
still, I will always be her and she will always be me, *too*.

> *When brought to daylight the same hour me and you*
> *(18)*

I live in you,
you live in me.

Home's a chimney
with you and me.

If I am one
you are half,
and half my one.

All you are is me,
all I am is you.

For all I have
belongs to you.

My all,
and all comes with it,
I share with you.

The life of mine and every
jot of me, I live for you.

And to breathe solely, *I do*
to harmony with only you.

O' Home's a spine, *my spine,*
carries me with you.

~

My heart was half a crooked heart
yours was born to mine, a perfect match.

My shape with yours fell into one hand
and made the one heart for me and for her.

Then they held onto each other for long
and your half promised me a life for so long.

The too wonderful a melody in your chest sang,
and I along.

My guessing my love when you went too young,
we settled not a life, but a song.

A song only you and I synced to tongue,
A song, *my love,* in heaven sung.

A Song Sung in Heaven
(17)

I want to wear you
If I must have you
as only air
when I seek you in vision.

I must become you
If I am to know
a life empty
of your unparalleled sight.

I shall remember you
If destiny recites for me
a living without the sound
of you breathing.

I do, with eyes seeing
and asleep, chastise air
for air, so, *so nothing*
could not endure the diamonds in you.

Thus, I must never stop
holding you in memory
and I, *forever,*
shall remember *you.*

I Want to Wear you
(17)

*B*lue hue made morning sky
Rove towards me, by and by
A vanilla sky in pearl blue dye,
Took from the color of your eye.

Come down at me, you lovely she
My eyes can't believe, it's you that they see
The skylight runs, carries you to me
You are the dream, *I still for be.*

Your eyes in love, graze in me
My tears well a long eighth sea,
The sky arrives dressed as she
Came to sew my heart for me.

Could it, my love, hurt you, *I plea*
The moment when you left me,
Nothing comes a word from she
But a cloud blink, *soft rain at me.*

The trickle mend my heart and I
Hold your hand before you fly,
You smile at me and *red and shy*
The blue is pink with your goodbye.

The Sky Is Pink
(22)

Red

The color of passion and desire,
True Love.

The Time Is Love

Love songs from here to sunrise
And a heart made for those eyes.
Man lose his wits and fool the wise
To gaze at the dream of you undies.
My lungs two birds frolic the skies
I have a thing, *my everly,* for your eyes.
No poet can near or can reprise

the poems I have for two of your eyes.

Poems I have for your eyes
(22)

I loved her everyday
And more so I today
My heart grows breadth by day
And I'll love you more next day.

I love her from afar
Name and gist, all you are
For all her glow my lids ajar
I am a man adore a star.

I lost my legs, my arms for you
My sense, my being, all blue
My mind went way, never back due,
Nothing but the eyes could, *too*
A heart enamored, from me to you.

A luster walks into my room
The parted lids an added bloom
My poor heart cease but then resume,
For the one mad feeling that I assume—
My sun willfully revives me from a tomb.

Thus, to love my love is to the sun
Can't I be certain, do so, *everyone*?
To gaze at you afar, a destiny, my sun
Gleefully, I clutch my ever so loved one,

Cast your light, and love, to I and to none—
Blind a man, my love, gazes too well, and stun
You are my breath, my only why, *my sun*
To love you from afar is fair, my fair one
And watch you from a star, *I do*, as you've done.

She's the Sun
(22)

To the moon is another face
Brighten the *dark* place.

Wide in the blue sky
To have seen him every eye
But baby my oh my
My moon is very shy
Run away the azure sky
And like a man come by.

My moon is only my
Need not I a sky
Lucid the day and nigh'
Forbidden is our goodbye
My moon is only my
Lighten the crook of my eye.

To the moon is a *man's* face
Bright and full and grace.

Blaze the iris of I
Glow both of my eye
The moon make leg and spry
Come to me as lullaby,
The sky is rain and dry
Her moon left and found a guy!

My moon come by and by
Baby, blue his eye
Shine the day, sail the nigh'
There's bleeding blue in the sky
Lost her moon and her pride,
Forgotten to baby, blue-eyed.

To the moon is *one* face
I am by him, *face-to-face*.

Baby, blue
(22)

*I*mmortal stars die alive
next to the color of her eyes.

No eye the color and use of man—
see, my love, what I swear I can.

At the meet of eye and I know why
foul in the world go and come by.

For hid and found in this world
one heaven for man to behold.

It is a fabulous place fashioned and furled—
the color of my love's eyes kissed and curled.

Shall bear the bane, and many, you and I
to heal, only, in *Spring Sky Blue Eye.*

~

My O'poor eyes, you fail to see, but only she—
her eyes craze, capture and so claim me!

~

The two pearl dyes of my love's eyes
make shy the stars, seas, all skies.

And how my long verse fails, as fluent tongue ails
her two March eyes, the verve breath takes.

For even the blue sky of day
by my woman's eyes grey.

And to live is to moment my love's eyes roaming,
for in the thrill of lost and found is a moment—

To look to a Spring Sky, *blue*, and notice
my love's eye closes and opens.

Spring Sky Blue Eye
(22)

Sweet dreams be made with she,
no one has or looks like he.
Sum of you and some of me,
I resign the half of that I be
for if all air, skies, stars agree
that in your eye a fond of me
forgo I will, eyes, ears, in glee,

*tell me, tell me all you love to see
is I with mine, my heavenly thee.*

Sweet dreams
(22)

The marry of summerspring air
Never regard, fancy or care
You kiss me then right there
And bloom sunflower in my autumn hair.

Syne, the universe with stars in love affair
My time cease and since my kiss, a December ne'er.

Summerspring flower in my hair
(22)

*H*ad she a beauteous Jane or just a plain
Had he the honor of man or false and wane
The whole world honest or is it all feign?
Shall the woman in me silly or sane,
That mustn't know until time or vain.

I have loved you since the open of time
Pit my love with the begin of rhyme
Us mustn't know truth from empty chime
If man the vile or worth the while,
It is only our love stand the test of hour.

Between us lovers and a whole world
A sea to die before the death of my word
To your dream eyes, *I verse,* and the daze of you,
No one can know my love to you not or true,
Except my love, the moment, and *me and you.*

The Time Is Love
(22)

Evergreen

The Color of life.

Somethings are life

Tonight, mine
Tomorrow, thine
Day, my; *Demain*, thy.

Shy the wild tide
return in polite pride
still, storm, side to side
to me glide, away reside.

Kneel for me and plea
remission, then once, flee,
C'est la belle, belle vie
Mon cher, cher ami.

C'est la vie
(22)

Between my tips and from behind
Blessing to miss, blessed too blind
It is but one, one fail to mind
The only one, one cannot hide
Two lucid lips, cannot describe
The earth, the river, a whole mankind

It is but one, destine, I remind
The magic to which, *one look to the sky.*

Magic Sky
(22)

*W*ane drizzle do the wild rain
I lave, sleep and drink the bane
Nay the thrill in self-inflicted pain

but the once to feel so vain,
to watch the skies, ever, make me sane.

Two haiku the rain
(22)

The jig of handsome maple leaves
The time each sways and barely weaves
Even when she droops and grieves
I long to jig-swing-cry underneath—

The sky could glisten in early spring
That milky-cloud a picture coloring
The rain a nightingale trickle and sing
O' to gaze at day again, *every, everything*—

The jolly parade of plenty people dance
Or walk or stand or doze and trance
Just the eye of blue, brown to glance
Give an extant life, a breath of romance—

Bring me a dream, the day I had before
The one I crumbled and thankless and bore
Trade today my day someday afore
Sweep closer, *April,* blow life in my hope—

April
(22)

*W*anders the wilt, awry hope
Sole slit from quest and cold
Dust thread on hair that's gold,

The heart, two arms open and hold
Wistful, whispers "to me come Home.."

Coming Home
(22)

Rose-Pink

The color of romance,
A blush on a lover's cheek.

Tales of Tongues Tied

*L*et me love you in a way
Word not know to say:

My life measured by day
One with you, another astray
A day by you, a day I weigh
The life of mine not by stay,
It is one, my love, which I say
I love you so & today
My life not count by *my* day
But the moment, *my love*, me & you, *hey*.

Birth of Day
(22)

I couldn't love you in words,
Only eyes.
I couldn't make this love
To the tongue of two,
I live for you, *I long for you.*

My lips,
A trap that trap,
Secrete and due wrap,
My so very adoring love—
Between me, the breeze and the sky, alive.

And for the hearing that never
Knew and flavored my heart,
You are
My one—
All I love.

My dearest *heart,*
If a silent love
Of silence die,
Mine eternal
Mine, *alive.*

Do you dream me, *my love*,
As I dream you,
Morn, eve and night.
These cosmos mean nothing
I only fantasy your loving.

Could I upon this love
Be a little mindless
I would call every human eye
All of you,
All the skies,

From heaven to bone
Earth to unknown,
To call you now or I will—*how*?
Your name, my love,
Would be as well, *mine*.

And of my weakness
Feed your heart
I swear mine restless,
Deathless,
Endless, *alive*.

Ample
Is
My silent love
For both your love
And always mine.

Had you perhaps spoken the words I close
You'd know your silent love mine, too.
I know, my darling,
I swear I do,
You can't breathe, *and I too.*

Thus,
Up till the day you and I and *breeze*
You and me come and leave
With lovers in our gazes,
The ones to die for, *we thieve.*

Never knowing what you are to me,
The ever restless
A moon, a star and me
All of us in love and nay sleep,

deprived dream, the where you are in love with me.

My silence, Love
(18)

*F*or how the earth made in me
Is shy and scared and O' how she
With hands velvet, delicate, but me
Too rough and ugly, *my hands*, to touch thee.

For how my heart jitters in a fever breast
I long to touch you, but fret makes home my chest
Battles, *he*, the tips, aches for you and unrest,
My coward heart beats myself at her best.

But, my only love, I breathe for two
To see my dream, and touch my dreams—are you
I have drowned in, the one woman I love, who
I cannot dare come close to.

O' near, nearer, the one I love, see
I am a man with a shadow fond of thee
Come close to and visit, a man in love—me
I'll introduce my shade to a marvelous she,

Already in love as much as me!

We'll set our shadows bold and free
Will let them do that we fancy and plea
My shadow will love, and so will I she,
Our ghosts will do what we wish we could be.

Le rendezvous des silhouettes
(22)

*G*reen eyed, he
brown eyes, she

"I wish more words could be"
"You have them all," she
"Would love it so to plea
for this in my heart to flee,
find a girl I love, O' she,
rustle all those things in me
flatter her, praise and see
home again, the heart of me."

Knowing smile, so lovely she
await more fond of green eyes he,
thus, the lips part and fount and sea:

"This won heart finished to she
so love and long and me
charmed and rivet and he
cannot yield but only to she,
revive the chest a look at thee."

The brown of eyes of she
hide and shy and glee,
the greenery eyes of he
bold and fond, and all three.

"Mine away, come with me
take my hand and jump and free
destiny to where sky meet sea
that shall be where I be
my heart there, and with you the key."

Avow great love too had she
as bright and big as that of he,
the eyes of lovers always be
stories and fairies on branch of a tree.

Thus, sung to her brown eyes had he,
crooned to his green ones, too she,
while the lips never spoke or be
ever close to *the eyes of we.*

I to eye
(22)

*I*n the everyday clouds, I look for you
rummage through the skies, deep, deep, blue
unravel each one to a day get to—
my life's pursuit, *you*.

In the evening stars, I watch for you
spring, one by one, to find my duo
reach out my tips to see how due
my touch meets yours, *I long for you*.

In all colors of eyes, I pursue
brown, green, grey, gold and blue
and every other tinge I would too,
I'm yours, *lonely*, come make us two!

My love is strong as death, as true
for I surely know nothing but those two,
I pledge all my hours to look for you
with eyes opened and eyes hue,

the dream is perfect and someone is too!

All I want is a day and who
might a night, could I electrify you,
to stroll the earth is too few
to find somebody to love you.

And to be loved by somebody, *anybody,* is you
I'll split the earth and find a view
the one I hoped for, my whole life, who

I am to die; die for you.

To die for
(22)

There's not a story that I could tale
That lived, my friend, without no ail.

Not one story that I could place
Without the love run or chase.

A plenty of love I've held and seen
Glow and Gloom, they both convene,
And I have died in each one I've been.

I've had a love once waited for me
And a love I waited for and dreamed
But a love for once had come for me
And made me forget each one of these.

Yet even that one come and leave
For also the sweet, sent must grieve
And I have died in each dawn and eve.

There's no story goes, my friend, awhile
Woes, wonders, wildflowers, but *I'll*
Be born again, when I see you smile.

Born Again
(22)

*B*ygone, bygone a time afore
Human were something more—
Dual the heads and limbs are four

The heart of man once a whole.

Ever, a half took his to the moon
Breast to breast, a piping tune
Twins the eyes, each other swoon

I am a man with my soul in two.

But *Jupiter* split my heart and you
For what could not we be and do
One soul, within the me and you

I am one half; you make us two.

But a thunder broke and my soul too
Had made the shape of exactly two
Lost with my lover, and my lover too

Grieves the earth for half of his who.

Then life became for us the two
And all the souls that heartbreak knew

To season and to mellow and somehow to do
The whole Earth back and someday due;

In pursuit of the only man who
Cupid arrowed in exactly two
I'll match my soul with half of two

And find my halved soul, body, avenue
To where my heart is full of you.

Soul-Searchers
(22)

*(inspired by the myth of soulmates
from the ancient tale of Aristophanes)*

Yellow

The color of sunshine,
Still breathing hope.

To love—is to and fro

*W*hat's in the world, a moment with you
Is a lover, his heart, mine too
Do men love, as women do
Or must one love, and the other *who*…

I love you the more, and the more I do
I wonder the ever, have you once too
The eyes meet, *ours both a blue*
I ask them, *charmed, had the love been true*…

He lost my mind, and nothing can undo
The malady is the medicine, the both are you
Thus, I crawl in the eyes, *a brighter blue*
I undress and dress, to be *like you*…

I swim in a suit and trip in brogue shoe
I look at two marvel eyes, *a darker blue*
I follow myself, from my lover's eye view
I wonder the ever, could you love *her* too…

Belle of the Ball
(22)

My love is one as the sea
Savor her once, and she
Will perfume better than to breathe.

Look at my lover and see
None but she rival the deep
One gaze and thy age fleet,
Sole flutter, and soul free.

My love is one as the untold sea
Competes the sky and only she
Beats her and flows— *through, in me.*

Nigh my lover, one breath, and see
My lover is one match the sea
Come closer, one foot, and thee
Shall fall or sink or *me.*

My love is love as the sea
Enchantress, Boundless, Everly
And as the sea can that be, she—

Ruthless, Lawless, Treachery.

My love is one as the sea
(22)

*H*ow so a time an earth sleeps
Man like me wakes, weeps

The world at rest, so calm her chest
As my lids agape and blink at best

They watch the universe steal my eyes
And decorate with, sleepless skies

Thus, my rainy skies for eyes
Watchers and wooers, undies

And from today I sight as do skies
I see all things, when day and when dies

I am there as the waves retreat
I am there when the ocean's eyes meet

I feel the sun comes fever day
And I shall feel her go dream and stray

Her moon bids day the bye, bye
Thin, thin to his day too, die, die

O' must also the stars go
Her friends doze, as does so

And as my bed breathes
Heavy when the night breeze

Stay by, my round gape sky
To think about you and why

Destined to love is I
And my love no drowse nor mine.

Eternal Eyes
(22)

I miss you more than I could do
breathe me away, somewhere to you

Save me as only one could do
or blow me to where I am to find you.

My day bleeds into a sun, sets and stolen
the night falls onto my heart, black and broken

I follow you, my star, only in the happy where
pursue you shan't in the counter do I dare.

Could my love see my eye spent and weary
for them they sleep—can't, dreamy and teary

Give me the die I so long for
just the hour, I wake and seek them more.

I die alive, and without you live to death
since you bare, sleepless is the breath

I find you none in my findings every day,
leave me the night to breathe once again.

Diaries
(22)

*N*ever once kissed, but twice
One man and that his vice
Shan't women desire a thrice,
To kiss me a never, or paradise.

My first, loved with eyes blue
Too dark, blinded me more than you
Gave love with all of that he knew
Enough to make life short for us the two.

My last, loved with a heart less by some
The beat of a lover's chest— drum, drum
The wiser a man in love— dumb, dumb
One must love plenty and for I, *numb*.

The love that once been— gone, gone
Two men loved and for I, none.

The love I never had— lost, lost
Two men loved till the heart exhaust.

> *Two men I never loved*
> *(22)*

Sing me, my love, how fairly could it be
when you *wonder-watch* the marvel of me
with stars for eyes, glisten and glee
like I am that, you were born to see.

Whisper, my love, how may and shall it feel
the merry or the misery from head to heel,
betray, my love, the riddle that you seal
is the sun or the storm in the bust you conceal!

Tell me, my love, how closely that you see
the one you love at times grey or green
sometimes in love, some eves just me
what could you pray for, or plea,

To win her or at best, for her to keep.

Cry, my love, how very you secrete
were I my love, I am artful and conceit,
for that the rosy smile that you deceit
ain't so sunny, ain't so sweet.

Yell, my love, how ever so you knew
my hand in yours, too morning dew
somedays dance, some eves just blue,
that your paradise, my love, was always due.

For to love her and to see all through
in a chest that hoped and heavied two
also in those eyes you always knew,
your love tries to fall in love with you.

ملاکی
(22)

*B*rief look in the mirror one day
You see my eyes a moment doesn't stay
You miss my arms wrap around your waist
And wish my eyes weren't gone so haste.

The passe love in glace dream
In the years to come by and by, we meet
See me again the heart skip a beat
Lament perhaps you a moment with me.

Photographs, the rest of you
Lapse as everything do
Faded face as if photographs knew
I shall lose you and they shall too.

But my heart had early sew you a face won't pale or go
She keep you yet as close a wind that friend and foe.
The cave you dug and go streamed with desert and woe
But know my love, sweet and slow I never writ at your hello;

I'll lay by the dim light vase
Trace your handsome face I'll dream of your embrace
And save you a seat wherever I place.

Breeze, breeze to and fro sway,
bring my love and timeless grace
Dazzle, dazzle come my way,
hope is a door crack, *just in case.*

Lovers' fate
(22)

*H*e fancy she
thus fancy he
the heart of man, facile foresee
for no one loved another be
with the next once, *short of thee.*

To love—is to and fro
(22)

White Light

A miraculous mixture of all colors combined.
White is all things, white is everything.

All colors of the rainbow

Shook the earth from underneath
The aim of life tickle my feet
A little girl in the meadow meet
The sense of life, O' so sweet.

Come, come, come at me
Hear her too, trembling tree
Bend and barrel and that would be
The poem that come chase after me.

The greenery of life and just me
Disturbed by poem and only she
Can drive up hell and set her free
To come flare through my rapid run feet.

Thunder through me, a lovely song
Hurry my mind and feet all along
To reach the stars and write lifelong
On skies the words where they belong.

But my oh my when the feet fail
A poem through me, bolt and bail
Too young to catch and blind to trail

Find another poet and leave me frail.
I feel her come, a sweet song versed
I run, I run, till the heart almost burst
I seize her at last and she would reverse
Find me, *and I*, from last word to first.

Ruth Stone
(22)

The God of breath, handsome breathe
Elle, la fille pour toujours vive.
Paint the day night and the night thieve
Breathe her a life, and deity conceive.

It is her, the one, mightier than sea
Man know and see nothing, just she
Not one can know or all of her see
It is her, *mistress of all*, you and me.

Summon the day and swallow the sun
At night birth the moon, for everyone
She's us all and without her can none,
Married the earth and lulled us one by one.

Opened her arms, *Nwt*, and I am to die
The earth, man and air together all sigh
Night the day and night to day, *and my*
It is she, in you and me, *a star filled sky*.

She Who Holds a Thousand Souls
(22)

The story of NWT,
The goddess of the sky, stars
and cosmos in ancient Egypt.

*I*n midnight poems I made
some *Wild Girl* portrayed
made me left, made her stayed—
a fierce, fast, fabulous jade,
a *Wild Girl* had made my trade

with a Jane, Poet, Lovely and Afraid.

Wild Girl
(22)

Strolled the earth its every way
The soft, the smooth and the splay,
Stomped the soils nearby and way
Strutted the decks on every bay.

Clutched the earth from tip to tip
Ranged her to the size of my hale grip,
Made every fortune touch my parched lip,
The freedom of man his master rip!

Treaded the green its every shade
Danced on her and my soul swayed,
When died the dye from my palm I paid
The earth, the garden for my feet I bade.

But O' when my hand aged and dried
My feet got angry for her stride,
Crushed my hand, arid eyed
And walked over me to find—

The hand that fed me a well wide,
But sea and sun, even tears I cried
Would keep the dead once have pride!

From greed to guilt a lonely man arrive

The sad years to the heart revive,
And on a day before the sun's last rise
My feet touch the green-colored surprise
A young rose I step, but she's alive!

Guilty Souls
(22)

The brain, the breast, fistfight,
The sense, the sentiment, in spite,
Shall I the sable, shall I the white.

The fight between a heart and mind
Scold my soul but sharp eyesight
Without the both, the rave & the right
The scream of reason, the gentle light
Man can never know a peace at night.

in Romance between the rave & the right
(22)

Orange

The color of freedom,
The one.

The light in my eyes,
The stars in the skies,
The sunset and sunrise

My darling woman, my dear man
None know me and none can
It is I, know nothing but the plan!

He, she, O' mighty sea, all frail
Destiny come, destiny hail

It is a calling whether to know
Him in triumph or wide woe
But it is a certainty, well to know

Him, the one, in that or tho'.

I know him in my heart
(22)

She seeks for you
With eyes you drew,
Two hands you knew
And a heart sworn for you.

Come find you her breast and sun
The moon, the earth, for everyone
The breath that made her and made them done
To love you is she, *and you her loved one.*

To you, her love, hurriedly hail
Run, run, sail, sail
The heart tremble and speak and swear
The loved one has, *always been there.*

Love Story
(22)

Violet

The color of dreams,
All magical moments.

Vent & Verse

*T*elling-tongues have gone dry
In a word of love and so am I,
A portrait of love at first eye
Masters mess, with colors don't dye.

For speeches of love and butterfly
Echo in empty and hollow sky,
And art and artists fail to imply,
The soul of my, all wooers and I.

Albeit, I'm no poet and much shy
And plenty of word lull with sigh,
Words at day the night deny
And nothing can capture or nearby,

Poetry or sculpt or lullaby
The sense I walk with and lie,
I'll sing, I'll paint and everly try
To declare my love, at first eye

Albeit, the latter, all else and I.

Albeit, I
(22)

Starlight
Star bright
First star I see tonight

Three wishes may
Three wishes might
Three wishes only for tonight.

~

My, my moonlight,
Give me, give me foresight
To know that may, that might
Only I and thy erudite.

O' in the daylight
I see the dark of the next night
The murk set on twilight
My life to come, blight!
Oh my Oh my, moonlight
I wish I may have or might
You rewrite my eerie midnight.

~

My lovely, dovely skylight,
For the second, give me delight
To bathe the every day and night
In a flare, golden sunlight.

O' in the hindsight
I bore and bore the spotlight
Allow me wander a handsome night
I long to fire and ponder about my knight!
Oh my Oh my, skylight
I wish I may have or might
Ache one night, my soul stir and ignite.

~

My so dearest candlelight,
My sweet, sweet tender light
For the last, gentle huff and goodnight
Close my eye and take away sight.

To-night the light
(22)

*T*he Pie Who Loved Me
tall and lean,
brown hair
and eyes almost green.

The Pie Who Loved me
a touch of he,
he *too* a taste of me
swilled me, like it's free
nothing more left of *she*.

The Pie Who Loved Me
a home close by,
between us just a thousand sea
in the middle, one lonely street
and a sky immortal, insincere.

The Pie Who Loved Me
gave me he,
all of him and none of me
grant me wings and cut my knees
loved me so well, *unloved by me*.

The Pie Who Loved Me
took my eyes, and now I see
your sad eyes, almost green
snuck my heart and slit it, *two, three*

I cry, an ocean and an empty sea.

The Pie Who Loved Me
took my name, and away from me
wilt my flower and set me free
darling knows he will see,
me and my eyes in every day, *dream.*

The Pie Who Loved Me
(22)

I crave oh crave the dim of night
I dart to meet the death of light
The day sink, the moon fright
His beloved sun, perish in sight.

She lulls away her darling groom
Never once doze her love to moon,
Sun hides away but her love bloom
My only sun in the sky, *mon amour*.

Midnight, midnight come find me
Bring her with the dull of thee
The grave of the hour dazzle but she,
Hear me pray or hear me dream.

Without her can live, but cannot be
Learned loving the hour you left me,
My silver midnight, bring me she
You are missing, my love, *missing from me*.

Tu me manques
(22)

I am a man's
and he is mine.
What could else
dream do I?

I am his
and he is my,
nothing can live
without you smile.

The day whirl
you and I,
a thousand years
to love your eyes.

With you no misery
nor no age,
to love you truly,
eternal grace.

Mine and his
(22)

Grey

Greyness was my timeless loss.

I love you, I love you, I love you…

*H*ad you taken me with you,
Never left me,
Told me our time be time,
So soon.

Had you blew me a farewell
I could understand,
Never left me,
The only faith I know
Wither until decay.

Had you warned my feeble heart,
I would train my eyes
They never know you again,
Briny tears a sole companion.

Had you whispered to me,
Promises of a soon assemble,
I could have made myself
One more time.

But
I would ache of anticipation
Rather
A burning separation.

Had only, you told me *my* fated day,
That I must,
See you anon.

I wouldn't have taken the sea,
We loved on so memorably,
My last sin

Where I escape to find you…

Sea, We loved on!
(17)

A smile gone too young
Sorrow sinks, fills my lung.

You leave me with—
The leaving of the sun,
She retires me with—
You, my beloved one.

Your fine, fine face, unexcelled
The life by us, I breathed, I smelled
Your lids finish the dreams I've held
Made day or daze, unparalleled.

The year we wed, just the last
Might make my agony pass the fast
For as with age fonders the past
I still live every day, the day you asked.

My wellness my lover, not soon
I promise you a misery, of mine and my moon
I shall not grieve you as my little time with you
My sad longing, live, from noon to noon.

The dying of a lover
(22)

I love you, I do
my love, know that true,
love never wither or rue
shall that love be with you.

My heart, one, endure
bold so in loving you
brave, I am, all through
from fancy to fond to woo.

My love had made me new
two flowers kissed by dew,
my flower pearl, yours hue
and a heart made in two,

one for me, one for you.
I know my love, I do
the pain that comes in queue
all love been, fall through.

But my love, I am to you
be, O' be mine too
know it a love one true,

I take the flame for a moment with you.

Permission to hurt me
(22)

I killed a man,
I kissed him
With poison lips,
I cage him

Inside my liar heart.

I whisper to him flicker of light
At darkest hour of lonely night
And rather than giving sight,
Blinded a man, too bright.

The possibility of she
Gave life and took from he,
The woman that was me
A mirage, could never be.

I saw you from the far
Eyes twinkle like a star
The dream of what we are
At the heart of his, a scar.

The break of me from you
A blow he wakes up to
The dream of me with you
Dies as all will do.

It killed a man, my lying
Of heartbreak, he's dying
My idle kiss, him flying
My changing heart, confining
Asking my name, he's trying
I lay by him, too crying,
I am *hope*, I kill, with you I'm dying.

It killed a man
(18)

The beauteous arrow that comes from me
A rose at end and a kiss summit thee

A shaft sturdy as the love you have for me
And a crest cragged as the one I have for he.

My lover got shot and the shooting bow is me
A kiss riddled the man that bends on his knee

A crimson rose dangles upon the heart of he
The crimson is red next to a blood make sea.

The pain made river and ran from she to he
As all the black blood came from my heart and me

His red rill, aflame, meets my mahogany sea
Black, bawling and boundless and no more we.

The love once been, spread mid you and me
My treason with your pain slather the soil and sea

I watch my guilt stain a sky, leaks a scarlet spree
The world pours my ichor and my tears go free.

~

But O' how this world loved you more than me
For the murderer in her made suffer three—

A day I've once lived, my lover's breath, and me

But as lovers die and eyes fill with plea,
The last breath goes to the reason of thee—

If I could live a day without the love of she,
Then save me you can't, *pray break me.*

Heartbroken by me
(22)

Steal my soul, my sweet, my so
Split my heart and don't you go
Stolen is one kiss I blow
As my lips to you I owe.

Hail, my love, seize that you own
You have me from skin, chest to bone
Come, my love, know what you've known
The garden you left turned into stone.

But a rose is left in the heart you broke
Come pick me, my love, she spoke;
I'll savor my slice and scent so nice
I'll plea my love to break me twice.

Rescue me and my so delicate a kiss
Might miss you, can't, more than this
Come, my love, my only bliss
My heart without you, fragile, *amiss*.

This misery, my sweet, is too my brain
Thus, to merry, my love, is to go insane,
For how lucky I'd be to storm and rain

And let my love *break my heart again.*

Heartbeat Is Heartache
(22)

This cannot be the first while
I tremble before her breasts
I seek to vet but that smile
 My swelter sense arrests.

She kisses me with her eyes
And tales and poems in mine,
 Forbye her gaze and her eyes
My mind is lost and not mine.

Each memory leaves me then all,
 She leans her palm to my chest
Amnesia like waterfall
Bathe me from brain to breast.

With one day spellbound eyes
My fine, fine fairy pierce my chest
Woe took her eyes that beguile
My captured soul smitten and unrest.

This spent heart, of mine, means to rift
 A vision grips he and crushes delicately
I surrender to she and the drowned adrift
The missed memory recurs.. ripples me.

My belle love draws my soul slowly
And I love her more to all times
She cries but I love her more, *mostly*
For how sweet she avenges and crimes.

At last, I watch some life ago
As one last breath I lastly blow
A similar heartbreak on the woman I adore
I have already done, and seen before.

Déjá vu
(22)

*F*or what shall that, reputed love be,
If that shall come and that shall flee?
But love is blind and lovers cannot see
And I've been blind with no love to me.
For what shall that, my passe loves be
Came and gone and always left me!
But the soul never let a thing go free,
A love without some successor to thee
Thus my soul conspires and brings me he.

The night my lover comes, finds me
My eyes confuse the sky with sea
I go to touch that, I go talk to thee,
But the sky shrivel and evade only me,
And a sea, cannot, cannot hear from she!
In the avenue from sky, also from the sea
The day is night, no man, not a tree!
But that one shadow never leaves me be
He softly thole and hold the hand of me.

To switch in bed, sadly left or de—
You drowse with, and come with me.
And if I leave you in the morning be
Must find me in the day would briskly he,
My lover once sidled, then weld with me.
Could love be measured by we

Lovers would ache and envious be
For half my loneliness I see in thee
And the other one lives, *always in me*.

The Solitude Soliloquy
(22)

*F*or how was one to know
this body is not our own
this spirit, no man's home
but you, and you alone

These bones refine to you
this soul, those arms, subdue
my tips, my marrow, adieu
remold all to you…

Yours, yours, all through
but O' just when they knew
my soul, my body, they flew
left me to breathe and love you

Had love been deity, but due
dries and woes and goes blue
my bones, my all and some, too
wander and wind, and *rendezvous*

They go, and go, adieu
take much of me and all -*you*-
my pieces chose, and I knew
they leave me when my love too

They love you more than once do
the woman they someday used to

Thus, I am without love,
residue.

Residue
(23)

Two wonder eyes wide for two
two mysteries, mystify and dew
dazzles, dreams, done and do
daisy days with and where you.

My eyes reverie and rendezvous
rove and roam to find you
when and where that is true,
crochet, color and craft you.

I dare and daze to touch you
arm in arm, each to each avenue
braided fingers, woven for two
braced hearts, I am to you.

My eyes glimmer, some light through
flutter and flicker, O' could I undo
from life to tale, my eyes rue
a dime I loved, had slipped through!

O' Sadness suit sight, when I lost you
thus sight turned fantasy, back to you
you are my dime, my to die for, do
my dime, my dime, fantasy or true?

Dime
(23)

*L*oving you is enough
loving you is enough

And being loved by you,
paradise.

To love you is to die the words
(22)

Black

Black is the absence of all color.

Forevermore;

*S*olitude of the night
Birthed in my chest
Spring to my bod',
Lonesome my daily ode.

My yesterday
A withered bouquet
Honest or gay,
Day end of the day.

My yesterday
Sky blue, and lover me and you,
Day was all day
And angel was all angel
Until her and I made a stranger.

I never once shied this paradise,
Myself an angel,
But I am here now
I am here how?

Thereafter,
The handsome dawn a vesper
Sunset upon her crown, *this angel*
Pierced her sworn of wing and glide
As her once charm a heart.

Eventide her name
Eventide her day
Eventide an angel.

Who is she,
Query angel
The dusk, the dawn

Who is angel?

Alone at sea
All known and beheld about she
Is not me.

I bled her
And afore your gore
I am angel
Later your losing,
Perhaps only I, and not angel.

My name
A silence,

And I am not the calling of the light
Me and the night left by an angel
Me and the night façade, *one.*

Angel and the night
(21)

*G*ood morning sun,
Good morning queen
The sun whispers
To my ear.

On a spring day we meet
I'm barefoot, I'm free
In the early day we see
The first of my life that be.
I were the rainbow
You morning color
I were your stranger
In secret you glance at me.

The summer noon breeze,
Less heat, more sweet
We tumble on our feet
We fall to our knees
We greet
O' like we're meant to be.
A stranger made friend
And for the summer we grew myrtle trees.

My former stranger made friend, gleams
With a face that glitters
And an eye that dreams.
My cully kisses me
And rhymes and beams.
On an autumn eve
My sweet reveals
His everly day to me.

O' Hail, hail, the night time
A winter storm, my door beats
It strike us both, I cover my feet
The rumble falls between you and me
She pulls our trees in the heartbeat.
This night I thunder, you lightning, repeat,
I see you for a time and the last
I know you again as someone I never have.

Goodnight day,
Goodnight grief
The moon holds and cradles me
Whispers goodbye before he leaves

And the sun next morning comes, finds me.

The life of a man
(22)

*L*et me none sleep
Let me learn the day from crest to deep
I shall nay sleep,
Sun, *moon*, meet, sweep

I, the middle, the ether, the both cheap,
Shall suffer the world and break to weep
Yay, never a minute *you* sleep, shall reap.

Let me none sleep
(22)

—Babe,
what once was had went, what is now be is
and what could have been is mine,
or almighty, his…

—my dear death speaks,
(22)

O' God well taught me or well punished me, he either well plagued me or well raised me, *to lose you.*
And today I am blunt in my sadness, polite in my asking, *today*
I am elegant in my pain.
Your loss is my deep, deep wound, and air is no healer but perfume. Your loss is my indefinite lesson, the truth I can never unknow, and the memory that will never pull me back together.
But I am still yours even if I tried, I am still somewhere there in me even if I smiled, I am still at heart yours for my smiles gone, *exiled.*
I am still yours, by thinking it was never worth losing you.

Nothing ever is
Nothing ever will be.

Lost on you
(16)

The wile of dusk,
The promise of dawn
Fool me at their duel of time.
Am I to morning,
Or the sapphire of the stars.

Between sunrise
Or a day that ever dies
Is only I, and a gullible sky.
Am I at farewell of twilight
Or a beholder to that one night,
Sacrifice and everly dwell light.

The skies cease to orchestra the life
The moment morn and eve fight
The field falls this instant quiet
The night, the light,
That may, that might.

عمری.
(22)

The End Is Blue

*The color of the infinite skies,
only at most times.*

I'll meet you again… where the field of fantasy meets life.

The End.

Thank-yous,

Writing this book has been more reward than labor, more belonging than longing and more me than I ever was.

To my family, thank you for believing in me and doing with me, for teaching me we have different eyes.
Still, I will always know in my heart that the things we're made of are just the same.

To my teacher, Reham Ali, you are more my teacher than school ever was, in the theater that's your class I loved to learn, I dreamed to do.
Thank you for inspiring me.

To Malak Hussien, the artist behind All the Colors of the Sky, thank you for your vision, thank you for your execution. You are a gem.

To my reader, thank you for being my most musical audience and staying through the mixtape of love
and life.

Malak